The Joy of Classics to Pops

Melodic gems from Baroque to Boogie.
Selected and edited by Denes Agay.

This unusual collection of wide-ranging themes, songs, and pieces is assembled and arranged here for all music lovers who enjoy every kind of good music, regardless of idiomatic labels. On these pages, echoes of the concert hall and opera intermingle with best-loved, most durable strains of Broadway and Tin Pan Alley; Bach and Mozart share the spotlight with Fritz Kreisler and Irving Berlin.

The Joy of Classics to Pops is truly a melodic feast, a musical smorgasbord to be savored by players and listeners alike.

Denes Agay

GW00685486

Order No. YK 21434
US International Standard Book Number: 0.8256.8073.5
UK International Standard Book Number: 0.7119.1279.3

Exclusive Distributors:
Music Sales Corporation
257 Park Avenue South, New York, NY 10010 USA
Music Sales Limited
8/9 Frith Street, London W1V 5TZ England
Music Sales Pty. Limited
120 Rothschild Street, Rosebery, Sydney, NSW 2018, Australia

Printed in the United States of America by
Vicks Lithograph and Printing Corporation

Yorktown Music Press
New York/London/Sydney

Contents

Hornpipe
from *Water Music*

George Frideric Handel

Badinerie
from *Suite No. 2*

Johann Sebastian Bach

Concertino Barocco on Themes by Handel
(Excerpt)

Denes Agay

Saint Anthony Chorale

Joseph Haydn
(harmonized by Johannes Brahms)

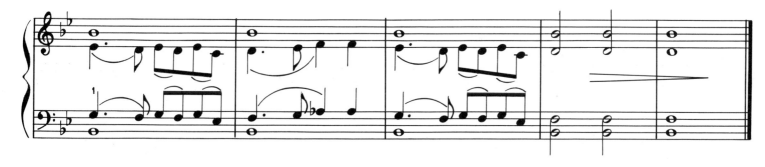

Air from Suite No. 5
"The Harmonious Blacksmith"

George Frideric Handel

Rondino
Theme from *Sonata for Piano Duet K. 521*

Wolfgang Amadeus Mozart

Minuet
from *Violin Concerto K.219*

Wolfgang Amadeus Mozart

Tempo di Minuetto

Fine

Impatience
from the song *Ungeduld*

Franz Schubert

The Trout
from the song *Die Forelle*

Franz Schubert

Liszt Gallery
Themes from Franz Liszt's *Hungarian Rhapsodies*

Arr: Denes Agay

* From Rhapsody No. 9 "Carnival in Pest."

Moderato con moto

ff eroico

* From Rhapsody No. 14

* From Rhapsody No. 6

21

* From Rhapsody No. 2

The "Fledermaus" Polka

Johann Strauss

March
Theme from *Symphony No. 6*

Peter I. Tchaikovsky

Themes from "Sakuntala"

Carl Goldmark

Rondo Alla Zingarese
Themes from *Piano Quartet Op. 25*

Johannes Brahms

Meno Allegro

Slavonic Dance No. 8

Antonin Dvorak

Slavonic Dance No. 10

Antonin Dvorak

La Campanella
(Caprice)

Niccolo Paganini - Franz Liszt

Love's Sorrow
(Liebeslied)

Fritz Kreisler

2nd time to Coda ✛

D.C.

Coda

dim. sempre

rit.

pp

Love's Joy
(Liebesfreud)

Fritz Kreisler

March Humoresque
(On A Ground Bass)

Edited: Denes Agay

Ernst von Dohnànyi

Allegretto marziale

Waltz Reminiscence

Dmitri Shostakovich

Waltzes
from *Der Rosenkavalier*

Richard Strauss

With a sentimental lilt

I'm Falling In Love With Someone
from *Naughty Marietta*

Rita Johnson Young

Victor Herbert

Mazurka
from *Masquerade* Suite

Aram Khachaturian

My Hero
from *The Chocolate Soldier*

Oscar Straus

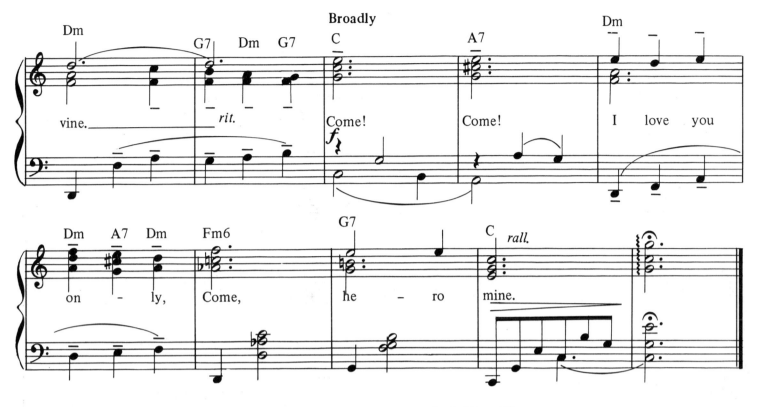

Oh, You Beautiful Doll

N. W. Ayer

A.S. Brown

School Days

Will. D. Cobb

Gus Edwards

School days, school days, dear old gold-en rule days, Read-in,' and 'rit-in' and 'rith-me-tic, Taught to the tune of a hick-'ry stick. You were my queen in cal-i-co, I was your bash-ful, bare-foot beau, And you wrote on my slate "I love you Joe" When we were a coup-le of kids.

When Irish Eyes Are Smiling

Chauncey Olcott
George Graff, Jr.

Ernest R. Ball

Danny Boy

Words by
Fred. E. Weatherly

Irish Folk Song

68

But when you come, and all the flow'rs are dying,
If I am dead, as dead I well may be,
Ye'll come and find the place where I am lying,
And kneel and say an Ave there for me;
And I shall hear, though soft you tread above me,
And all my grave will warmer, sweeter be,
For you will bend and tell me that you love me,
And I shall sleep in peace until you come to me.

Let Me Call You Sweetheart

Beth Slater Whitson

Leo Friedman

Some Of These Days

Sheldon Brooks

Alexander's Ragtime Band

Irving Berlin

Come on and hear, _____ Come on and hear _____ Al - ex - an -der's Rag time Band. _____

Come on and hear, _____ Come on and hear _____ It's the

best band in the land. _____ They can play a bu-gle call like you

nev - er heard be-fore, So nat - ur-al that you want to go to war;

That's just the best - est band what am,

Harmony Rag

Hal Nichols

I Wonder Who's Kissing Her Now

Will M. Hough
Frank R. Adams

Joe E. Howard

Slow waltz tempo

I wonder who's kiss - ing her now,

Won - der who's teach - ing her how,

Won - der who's look - ing in - to her eyes,

My Melancholy Baby

George Norton
Ernie Burnett

Rather slow

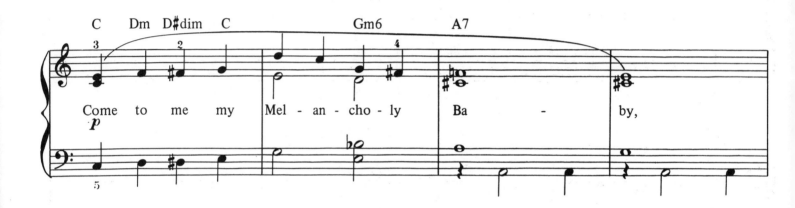

Come to me my Mel - an - cho - ly Ba - by,

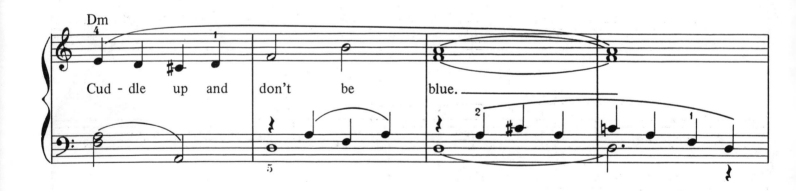

Cud - dle up and don't be blue. _____

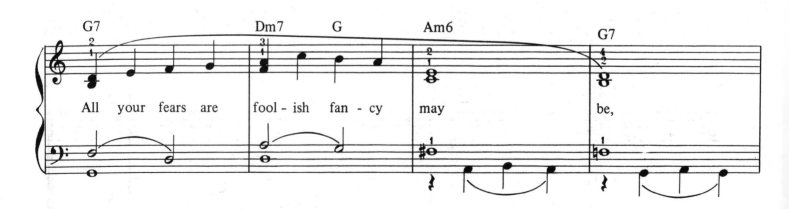

All your fears are fool - ish fan - cy may be,

The Casey Jones Boogie

Eddie Newton
T. Lawrence Seibert

Moderately